1

LET'S GO

Student Book

by
R. Nakata
K. Frazier

with

songs by Carolyn Graham

Oxford University Press

Oxford University Press

198 Madison Avenue
New York, NY 10016

Great Clarendon Street
Oxford OX2 6DP England

Oxford New York
Athens Auckland Bangkok Bogota Bombay Buenos Aires
Calcutta Cape Town Dar es Salaam Delhi Florence Hong Kong
Istanbul Karachi Kuala Lumpur Madras Madrid Melbourne
Mexico City Nairobi Paris Singapore Taipei Tokyo Toronto Warsaw

and associated companies in
Berlin Ibadan

OXFORD is a trademark of Oxford University Press.

ISBN 0-19-434393-6

Copyright © 1992 by Oxford University Press.

Library of Congress Cataloging-in-Publication Data
Nakata, R. (Ritsuko)
    Let's go 1, student book / R. Nakata, K. Frazier ; songs by Carolyn Graham.
      p.   cm. —(Let's go)
    Summary: A textbook for students learning English as a foreign
language.
    ISBN 0-19-434393-6
    1. English language—Textbooks for foreign speakers—Juvenile
literature. [1. English language—Textbooks for foreign speakers.]
I. Frazier, K. (Karen) II. Graham, Carolyn.   III. Title.
IV. Series.
PE1128.N25   1991
428.2'4—dc20   90-48027
                                                    CIP
                                                    AC

Senior Editor: Shelagh Speers
Designer: April Okano
Art Buyer/Picture Researcher: Paula Radding
Production Controller: Abram Hall

Cover design by April Okano
Cover illustrations by Paul Meisel and Patrick Merrell

Continuing characters illustrated by Dora Leder. Other
interior illustrations by David Cain, Kim Wilson Eversz,
Maj-Britt Hagsted, Steve Henry, Anne Kennedy, Paul Meisel,
Patrick Merrell, Bob Rose, and Maggie Swanson.

Printing (last digit): 20 19 18

Printed in Hong Kong

Icons

Every unit in *Let's Go* is divided into seven lessons, with additional review after every two units. Each lesson is identified by a colorful icon. The same icons are used for reference on corresponding pages in the Teacher's Book and Workbook.

Let's Talk
Functional dialogue

Let's Learn the Alphabet
Alphabet work

Let's Sing
Interactive song based on the dialogue

Let's Move
Classroom commands and action verbs

Let's Learn
New grammatical structure

Let's Listen
Listening test and unit review

Let's Learn Some More
Related grammatical structure

Let's Review
Further review after every two units

Table of Contents

Unit One

 Let's Talk

What is your name?
My name is John.

What is = What's

 **Let's Sing**

Andy

Jenny

Lisa

Scott

♪ **The Hello Song**

Hello, hello, hello!
What's your name?
Hello, hello, hello!

My name is John.
My name is John.

Hello, John!
Hello, John!
Hello!

Kate

John

7

Let's Learn

What is this?
It is a ruler.

What is = What's
It is = It's

Practice.

a book

a desk

a chair

a ruler

a pencil

a bag

a pen

an eraser

9

Let's Learn Some More

Is this a bag?
Yes, it is.
No, it is not.

is not = isn't

Play a game.

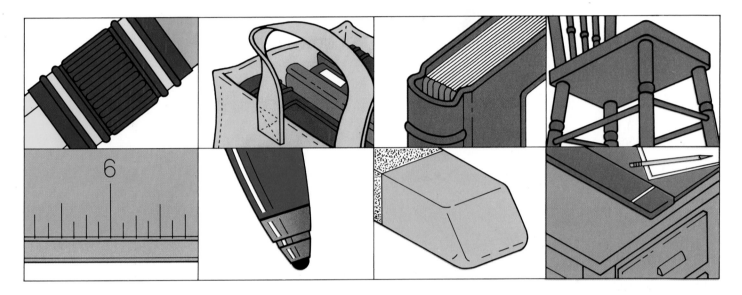

 Let's Learn the Alphabet

♪ **The Alphabet Song**

A B C D E F G H

I J K L M N O P

Q R S T U V W X Y Z

I like English!

Let's Move

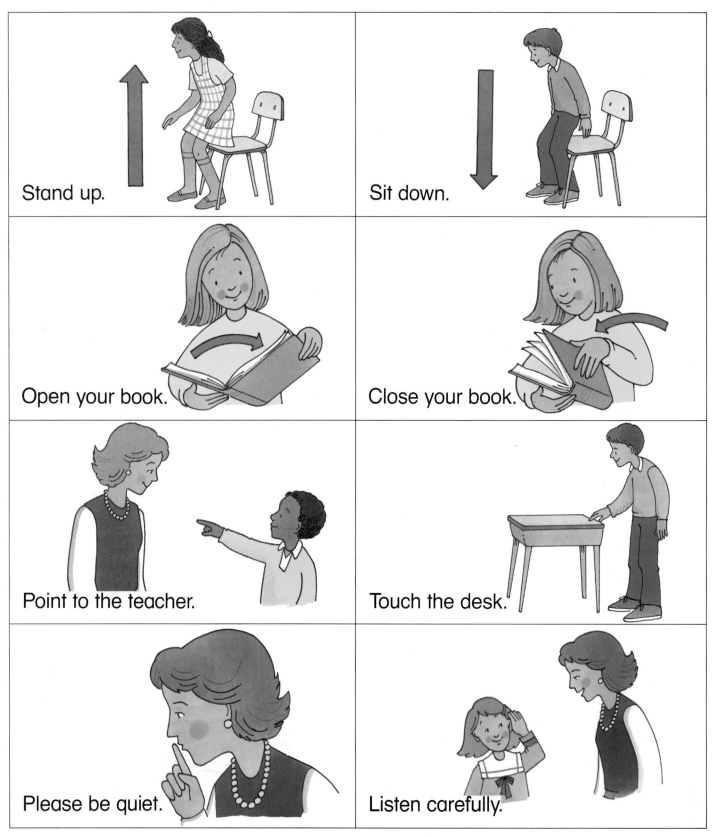

Stand up.

Sit down.

Open your book.

Close your book.

Point to the teacher.

Touch the desk.

Please be quiet.

Listen carefully.

 **Let's Listen**

1.

2.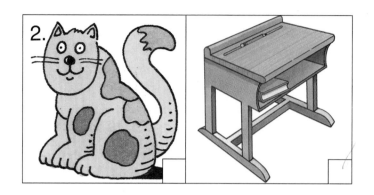

3.

4.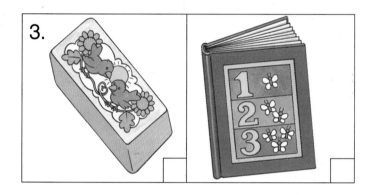

5.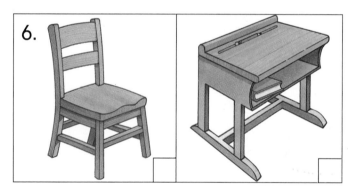

6.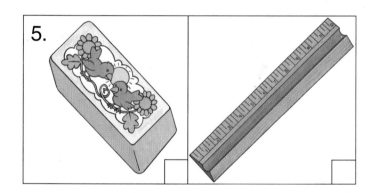

7.

8.

Let's Talk

Hi, Andy. How are you?

I'm fine. How are you?

I'm fine. Thank you.

How are you?
I am fine. Thank you.

I am = I'm

 # Let's Sing

♪ **Hi, How Are You?**

Hi, how are you?
   I'm fine.
Hi, how are you?
   I'm fine.
Hi, how are you?
   I'm fine. How are you?
I'm fine, I'm fine, I'm fine.

Let's Learn

What color is this? It is red.	It is = It's

Practice.

yellow	blue	white	pink	gray
red	black	green	purple	orange

brown

♪ **The Black Cat Song**

Let's Learn Some More

This is a blue book.
This is a red and yellow book.

Say these.

 Let's Learn the Alphabet

A a apple	**B b** book	**C c** cat

a b c d e f g h i j k l m n o p q r s t u v w x y z

 # Let's Move

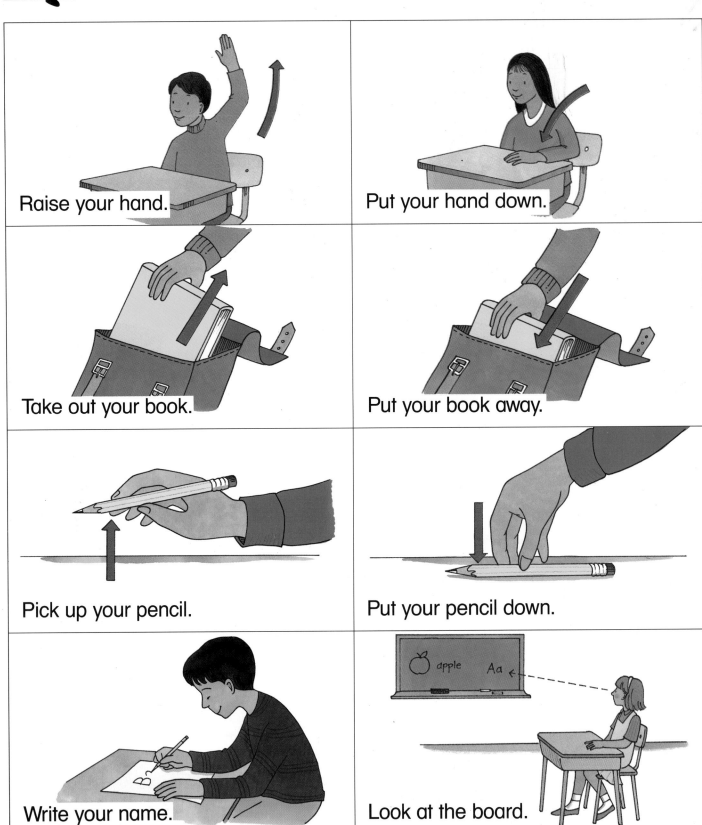

Raise your hand.

Put your hand down.

Take out your book.

Put your book away.

Pick up your pencil.

Put your pencil down.

Write your name.

Look at the board.

Let's Listen

1.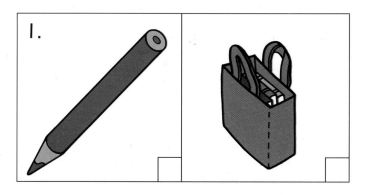

2.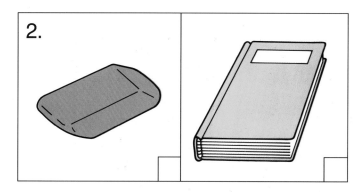

3.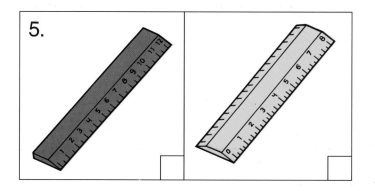

4.

5.

6.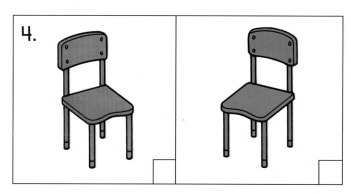

7.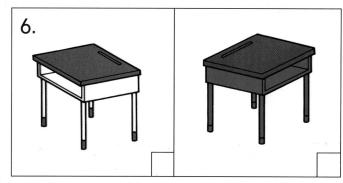

8.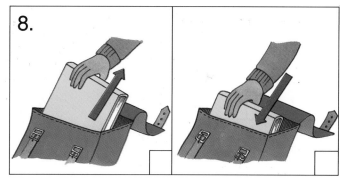

Let's Review

1. Say these.

2. Play a game.

What color is this?

It is _____.

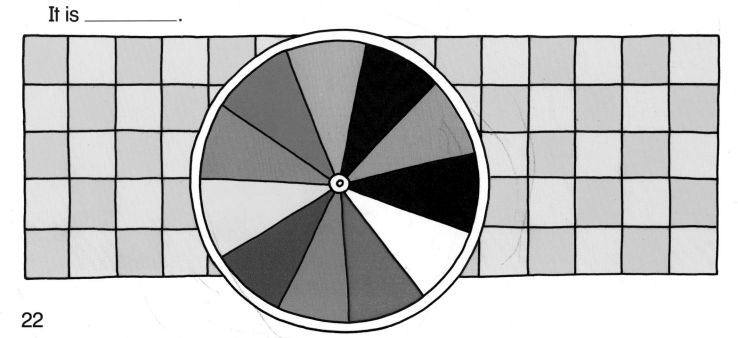

3. Say and act.

4. Ask your partner.

What is this?
Is this a _____?

5. Listen carefully.

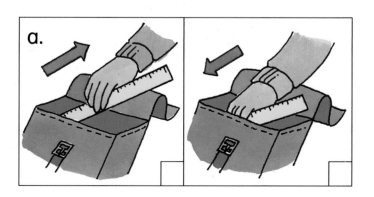

Unit Three

Let's Talk

This is my friend, Sarah.
Hello, Sarah.

Let's Sing

♪ **This Is My Friend**

This is my friend, Sarah.
   Hello, Sarah.
This is my friend, Sarah.
   Hello, Sarah.

This is my friend, John.
   Hi, John!
This is my friend, John.
   Hi, John!

This is my friend, Sarah.
This is my friend, John.
Let's play!

25

Let's Learn

What are these?
They are cassettes.

They are = They're

26

Practice.

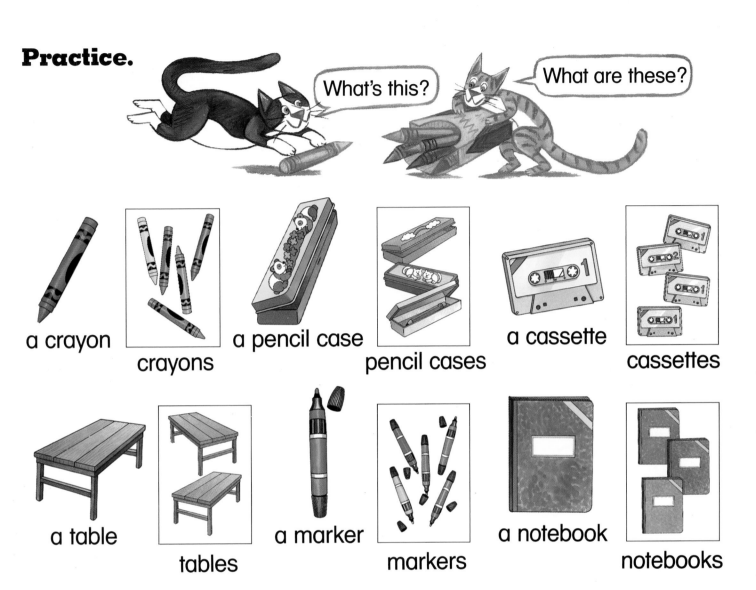

What's this?

What are these?

a crayon — crayons

a pencil case — pencil cases

a cassette — cassettes

a table — tables

a marker — markers

a notebook — notebooks

Say these.

This is a _____. These are _____.

27

Let's Learn Some More

♪ **The Purple Sneaker Song**

1   one

2   two

3   three

4   four

5   five

6   six

7   seven

8   eight

9   nine

10   ten

How many sneakers?

| One sneaker. | Four sneakers. | Seven sneakers. |

Practice.

How many cassettes?

Three cassettes.

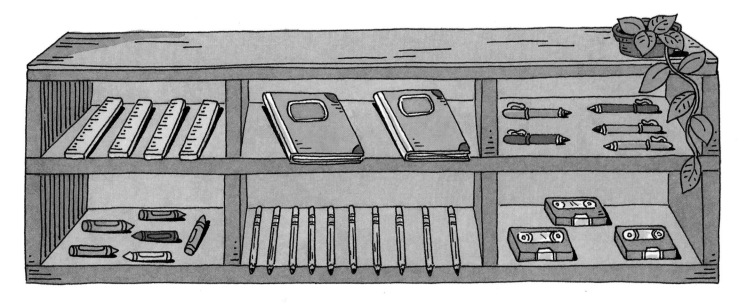

Let's Learn the Alphabet

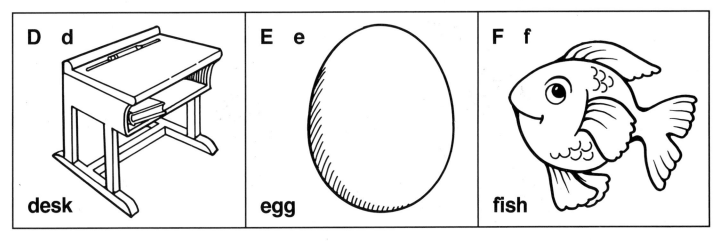

D d
desk

E e
egg

F f
fish

a b c **d e f** g h i j k l m n o p q r s t u v w x y z

 # Let's Move

Make a circle.

Make two lines.

Go to the door.

Come here.

Count the girls.

Count the boys.

Draw a picture.

Give me the crayon.

Let's Listen

1.

2.

3.

4.

5.

6.

7.

8.

Let's Talk

It is nice to meet you.
It is nice to meet you, too.

It is = It's

Let's Sing

♪ The Family Song

This is my mother.
    Nice to meet you.
Nice to meet you, too.

This is my father.
    Nice to meet you.
Nice to meet you, too.

This is my sister.
    Nice to meet you.
Nice to meet you, too.

This is my brother.
    Nice to meet you.
Nice to meet you, too.

Let's Learn

Who is she?
    She is my grandmother.

Who is he?
    He is my grandfather.

Who is = Who's
She is = She's
He is = He's

Ask your partner.

mother

sister

grandmother

baby sister

father

brother

grandfather

friend

Who's he?

He's my father.

Say these.

_____ is my sister.   _____ is my friend.

Let's Learn Some More

He's tall. She's short.

He is tall.
She is short.

He is = He's
She is = She's

Practice. He's young.   She's old.

young   old   tall   short   pretty   ugly   thin   fat

Guess.

She is old.
She is pretty.
Who is she?

She is my _____.

He is short.
He is ugly.
Who is he?

He is my _____.

He is tall.
He is thin.
Who is he?

He is my _____.

She is young.
She is fat.
Who is she?

She is my _____.

 Let's Learn the Alphabet

| G g  girl | H h house | I i ink | J j jump rope |

a b c d e f **g h i j** k l m n o p q r s t u v w x y z

Let's Move

go to sleep

Good night!

wake up

Good morning!

do homework

eat dinner

make a mess

clean up

watch TV

play the piano

Do not watch TV.

Do not = Don't

Don't watch TV.

Don't make a mess.

Let's Listen

1.

2.

3.

4.

5.

6.

7.

8.

Let's Review

1. Say these.

10 POINTS

2. Ask your partner.

Who is he?
Who is she?

Who's he?

He's my father. He's tall.

3. Say and act.

Hello, Sarah.

It's nice to meet you.

4. Answer the question.

How many _____?

5. Listen carefully.

Let's Talk

How old are you? I am seven years old.	I am = I'm

 **Let's Sing**

♪ **The Happy Birthday Song**

It's my birthday today.
    It's your birthday today.
It's my birthday today.
    Happy birthday, Jenny!

One, two, three, four, five, six,
    Seven years old!

Now I'm seven years old.
    Now you're seven years old.
Now I'm seven years old.
    Happy birthday, Jenny!

Let's Learn

What is it?
    It is a doll.

It is = It's

Practice.

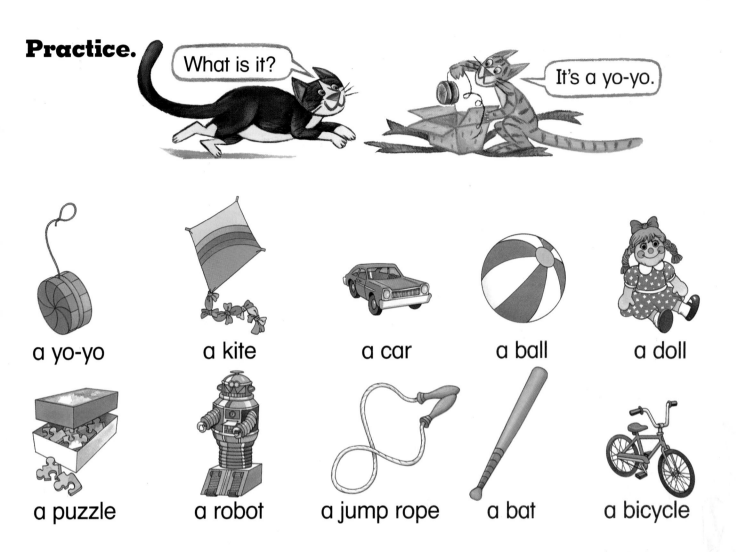

"What is it?"

"It's a yo-yo."

a yo-yo

a kite

a car

a ball

a doll

a puzzle

a robot

a jump rope

a bat

a bicycle

Guess.

What is it?

Let's Learn Some More

It is little.
It is a little yo-yo.

It is = It's

Say these.

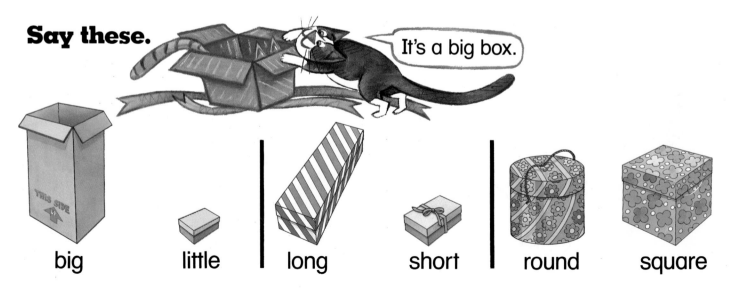

big   little   long   short   round   square

Practice.

Is it a pencil?

Yes, it is. It's a long pencil.

 Let's Learn the Alphabet

K k — kite

L l — lion

M m — mother

N n — notebook

a b c d e f g h i j k l m n o p q r s t u v w x y z

Let's Move

play with a yo-yo

throw a ball

catch a ball

hit a ball

do a puzzle

jump rope

Can you play with a yo-yo?
Yes, I can.
No, I cannot.

cannot = can't

Can you play with a yo-yo?

Yes, I can.

No, I can't.

Let's Listen

1.

2.

3.

4.

5.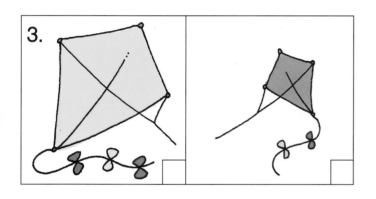

6.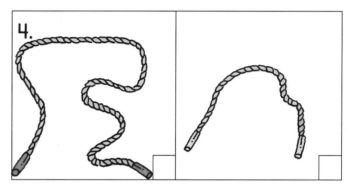

7.

8.

Let's Talk

How is the weather?
It is sunny.

How is = How's
It is = It's

♪ **How's the Weather?**

How's the weather?
   It's sunny.
How's the weather?
   It's sunny.
How's the weather?
   It's sunny. It's sunny today.

rainy windy cloudy snowy

51

Let's Learn

How many clouds are there?
    There are six clouds.
    There is one cloud.

There is = There's

Practice.

How many flowers are there?

There's one flower.

a flower   flowers

a tree   trees

a cloud   clouds

a puddle   puddles

Count them.

There is _____. There are _____.

Let's Learn Some More

in

on

under

by

Where's the kite?

It's in the tree.

Where are the books?

They're under the table.

Where is the kite?
    It is in the tree.
Where are the books?
    They are under the table.

Where is = Where's
It is = It's
They are = They're

Practice.

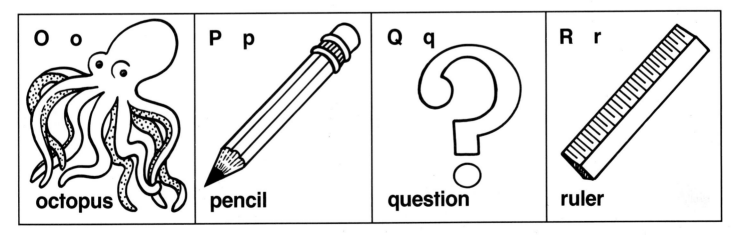

ABC/abc Let's Learn the Alphabet

| O o octopus | P p pencil | Q q question | R r ruler |

a b c d e f g h i j k l m n **o** **p** **q** **r** s t u v w x y z

55

Let's Move

climb a tree

play baseball

read a book

play tag

ride a bicycle

fly a kite

Can he climb a tree?
Yes, he can.
No, he cannot.

cannot = can't

Can he climb a tree?

Yes, he can.

No, he can't.

Let's Listen

1.

2.

3.

4.

5.

6.

7.

8.

Let's Review

1. Say these.

10 POINTS

2. Answer the question.

How many _____ are there?

3. Say and act.

How old are you?

?

It's rainy.

58

4. Ask your partner.

Can you _____ ?

Yes						
No						

5. Listen carefully.

Where is it?

a.

b.

c.

d.

Let's Talk

Here you are.
Thank you.
You are welcome.

You are = You're

Let's Sing

♪ **Peaches, Apples, and Plums**

Peaches, apples, and plums.
Peaches, apples, and plums.

What do you want?
I want an apple.

Peaches, apples, and plums.

What do you want?
    I want ice cream.
    I want cake and ice cream.

Practice.

milk

fish

chicken

pizza

bread

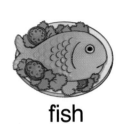

rice

cake

ice cream

Say these.

I want _____ and _____ .

Let's Learn Some More

Do you want chicken?
Yes, I do.
No, I do not.

do not = don't

Practice.

 Let's Learn the Alphabet

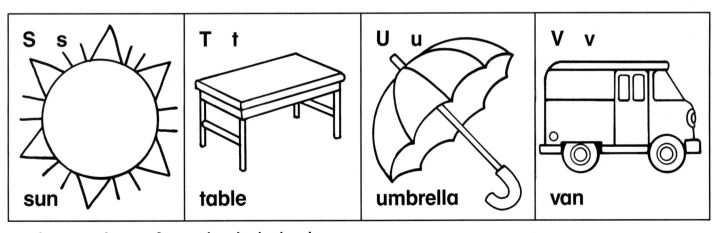

S s — sun

T t — table

U u — umbrella

V v — van

a b c d e f g h i j k l m n o p q r s t u v w x y z

Let's Move

| buy an apple | wash it | cut it | eat it |

| buy juice | open it | pour it | drink it |

Can you drink it?

Can you eat it?

Let's Listen

1.

2.

3.

4.

5.

6.

7.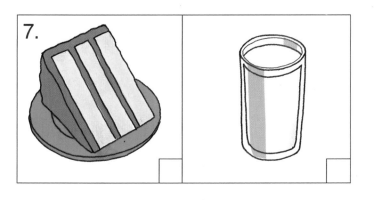

8.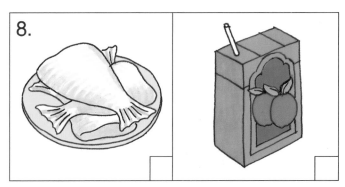

Let's Talk

What is your favorite color?
Red.

What is = What's

♪ What Do You Like?

I like yellow, yes I do.
I like yellow, yes I do.
I like yellow.
    I do, too.
    I like yellow, too.

I like ice cream, yes I do.
I like ice cream, yes I do.
I like ice cream.
    I do, too.
    I like ice cream, too.

I like baseball, yes I do.
I like baseball, yes I do.
I like baseball.
    I do, too.
    I like baseball, too.

Let's Learn

What do you like?
I like frogs.
I like frogs, too.

Practice.

There's a bird.
I like birds.

I like birds, too.

a bird	birds	a dog
dogs	a cat	cats

a frog	frogs	a rabbit
rabbits	a spider	spiders

Ask your partner.

What do you like?

Let's Learn Some More

Do you like spiders?
Yes, I do.
No, I do not.

do not = don't

Practice.

 Let's Learn the Alphabet

W w	X x	Y y	Z z
window	x-ray	yo-yo	zero

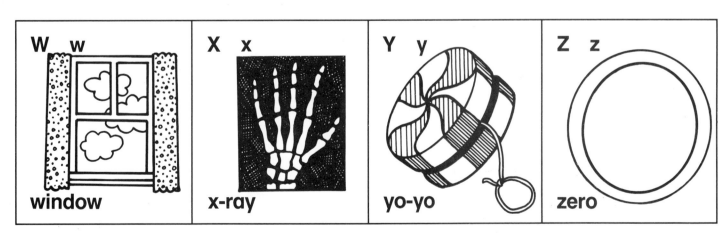

a b c d e f g h i j k l m n o p q r s t u v w x y z

 # Let's Move

walk

run

swim

fly

hop

jump

Can it run?
Yes, it can.
No, it cannot.

cannot = can't

Can it run?

Can it fly?

Can it swim?

Can it hop?

Let's Listen

1.

2.

3.

4.

5.

6.

7.

8.

75

Let's Review

1. Say these.

10 POINTS

2. Answer the question.

What do you want?

76

Say and act.

4. Ask your partner.

Do you like _____?

Yes							
No							

5. Listen carefully.

Let's Go 1 Syllabus

UNIT	LANGUAGE ITEMS	FUNCTIONS	TOPICS
1	Hello, I am (Andy). Hi! My name is (Kate). What's your name? What's this? It's (a book). Is this (a book)? Yes, it is. No, it isn't.	Greetings Introducing yourself Asking someone's name Asking about objects (singular) Identifying objects (singular) Classroom commands	Names Classroom objects
2	How are you? I'm fine. Thank you. What color is this? It's (red). This is a (blue) (book). This is a (red) and (yellow) book.	Greetings Asking about colors Identifying colors Describing objects Classroom commands	Colors Classroom objects
3	This is my friend, (Sarah). Hello, (Sarah). Let's play. What are these? They're (cassettes). How many (sneakers)? (Ten) (sneakers).	Introducing friends Suggesting an activity Asking about objects (plural) Identifying objects (plural) Asking about numbers Counting 1–10 Classroom commands	Numbers 1–10 Classroom objects
4	Hi, Mom! I'm home. This is my (mother). It's nice to meet you. It's nice to meet you, too. Who's (she)? (She's) my (grandmother). (She's) (short). Don't (watch TV).	Introducing family members Meeting someone politely Asking about people Identifying people Describing people Negative commands	Family
5	Happy birthday, (Jenny)! How old are you? I'm (seven) years old. This is for you. It's (my) birthday today. What is it? I don't know. It's (little). It's a (little) (yo-yo). Can you (play with a yo-yo)? Yes, I can. No, I can't.	Birthday greetings Asking and telling age Giving a gift Guessing Describing objects Asking about ability	Birthdays Age Toys

UNIT	LANGUAGE ITEMS	FUNCTIONS	TOPICS
6	How's the weather today? It's (sunny). How many (clouds) are there? There are (six) (clouds). There's one (cloud). Where's the (kite)? It's (in) the tree. Where are the (books)? They're (under) the (table). Can (he) (climb a tree)? Yes, (he) can. No, (he) can't.	Asking about the weather Describing the weather Counting Describing a situation Asking about location Specifying location Asking about ability	Weather Outdoor activities
7	I'm (hungry). I want (an apple). Here you are. Thank you. You're welcome. What do you want? I want (cake) and (ice cream). Do you want (chicken)? Yes, I do. No, I don't. Buy (an apple). (Wash) it.	Expressing hunger and thirst Asking what someone wants Expressing wants Logical sequencing	Food and drink
8	What's your favorite color? (Red). What about you? I like (blue). What do you like? I like (frogs). I like (frogs), too. Do you like (spiders)? Yes, I do. No, I don't. Can it (swim)? Yes, it can. No, it can't.	Asking about favorites Expressing likes Agreeing Asking about ability	Favorite colors Animals

Word List

A

a 8
about 68
am 6
an 9
apple 19
are 14
at 20

B

baby 35
bag 9
ball 45
baseball 56
bat 45
be 12
bicycle 45
big 46
bird 71
birthday 42
black 17
blue 17
board 20
book 9
boy 30
bread 63
brother 33
brown 17
buy 66
by 54

C

cake 62
can 48
cannot 48
car 45
cassette 26
cat 8
catch 48
chair 9
chicken 63
circle 30
clean up 38
climb 56
close 12
cloud 52
cloudy 51
color 16
come 30
count 30
crayon 27
cut 66

D

desk 9
dinner 38

do homework 38
dog 70
doll 44
don't 38
door 30
draw 30
drink 66

E

eat 38
egg 29
eight 28
English 11
eraser 9

F

fat 36
father 33
favorite 68
fine 14
fish 29
five 28
flower 53
fly 56
for 42
four 28
friend 24
frog 70

G

girl 30
give 30
go to 30
good morning 38
good night 38
grandfather 34
grandmother 34
gray 17
green 17
guess 45

H

hand 20
Happy birthday 42
he 34
hello 6
here 30
hi 6
hit 48
home 32
homework 38
hop 74
house 37
how 14
hungry 60

I

I 6
ice cream 62
in 54
ink 37
is 6
isn't 46
it 8

J

juice 60
jump 48
jump rope 37

K

kite 45
know 44

L

let's 24
like 11
lines 30
lion 47
little 46
long 46
look 20

M

make 30
many 28
marker 27
me 30
meet 32
mess 38
milk 63
mother 32
my 6

N

name 6
nice 32
nine 28
no 10
not 38
notebook 27

O

octopus 55
OK 50
old 36
on 54
one 28
open 12
orange 17

P

peach 61
pen 9
pencil 9
pencil case 26
piano 38
pick up 20
picture 30
pink 17
pizza 63
play 24
please 12
plum 61
point to 12
pour 66
pretty 36
puddle 53
purple 17
put away 20
put down 20
puzzle 45

Q

question 55
quiet 12

R

rainy 51
raise 20
rabbit 71
read 56
red 16
rice 63
ride 56
robot 42
rope 48
round 46
ruler 8
run 74

S

seven 28
she 34
short 36

sister 33
sit down 12
six 28
sleep 38
sneaker 28
snowy 51
spider 65
square 46
stand up 12
sunny 50
swim 74

T

table 27
tag 56
take out 20
tall 36
teacher 12
ten 28
thank you 14
the 12
there 70
these 26
they 55
thin 36
thirsty 60
this 8
three 28
throw 48
today 43
too 32
touch 12
tree 53
TV 38
two 28

U

ugly 36
under 54

V

van 65

W

wake up 38
walk 74
want 60
wash 66
watch 38
weather 50
welcome 60
what 6
where 54
white 17
who 34

window 73
windy 51
with 48
wow 42
write 20

X

x-ray 73

Y

years 42
yellow 17
yes 10
yo-yo 45
you 14
young 36
your 6

Z

zero 73